Fashion Fun

Coloring Book

Marjorie J McDonald

Introduction

If you want to be a clothing designer this is the book for you to help you get started with your sketching and color skills. Designing is a skill that can be obtained through simple steps. These steps require some action on your part be it to think a certain way, to act or react a certain way, or to take physical action. In reality, it takes a good balance of creativity and learning to draw well enough to be able to illustrate your end garment.

These sketches you can practice with and color in are from my ready to wear ladies dress line. Enjoy and have fun coloring them.

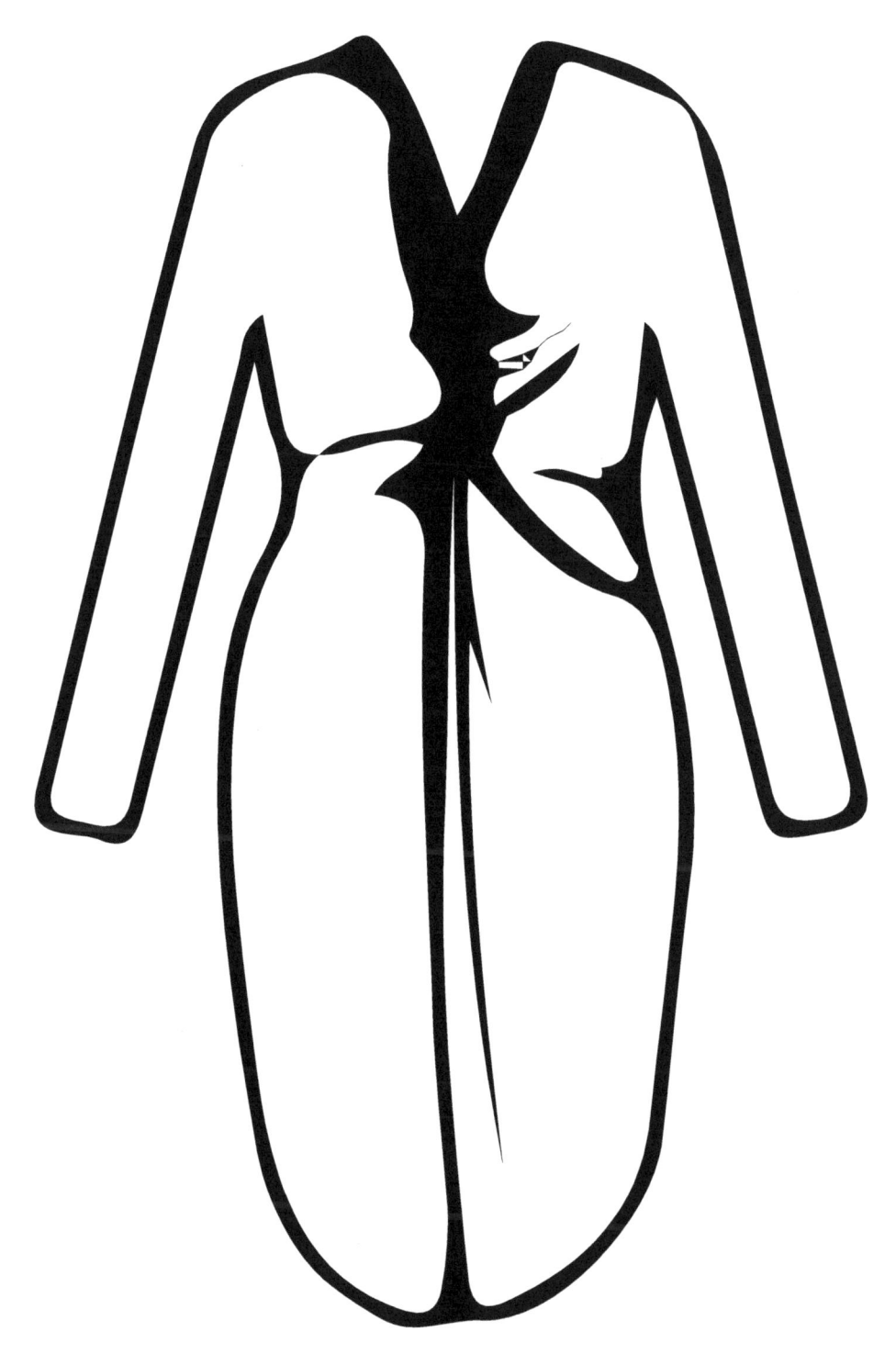

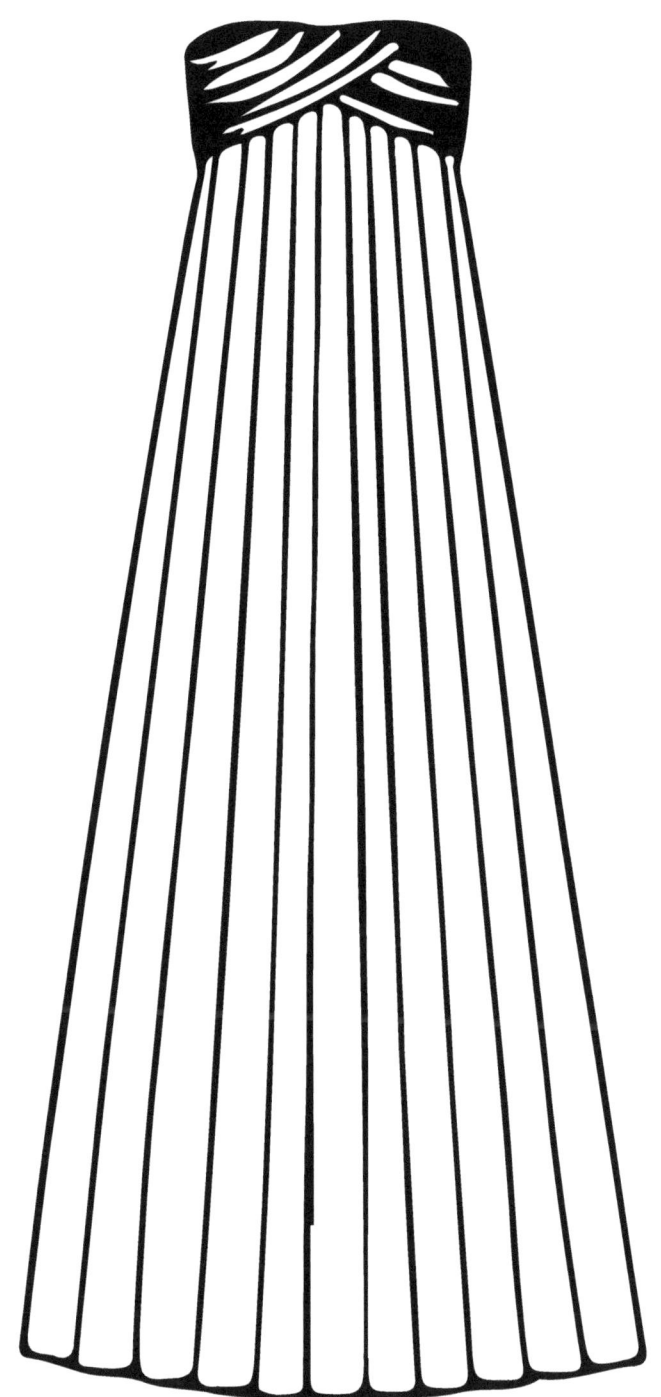

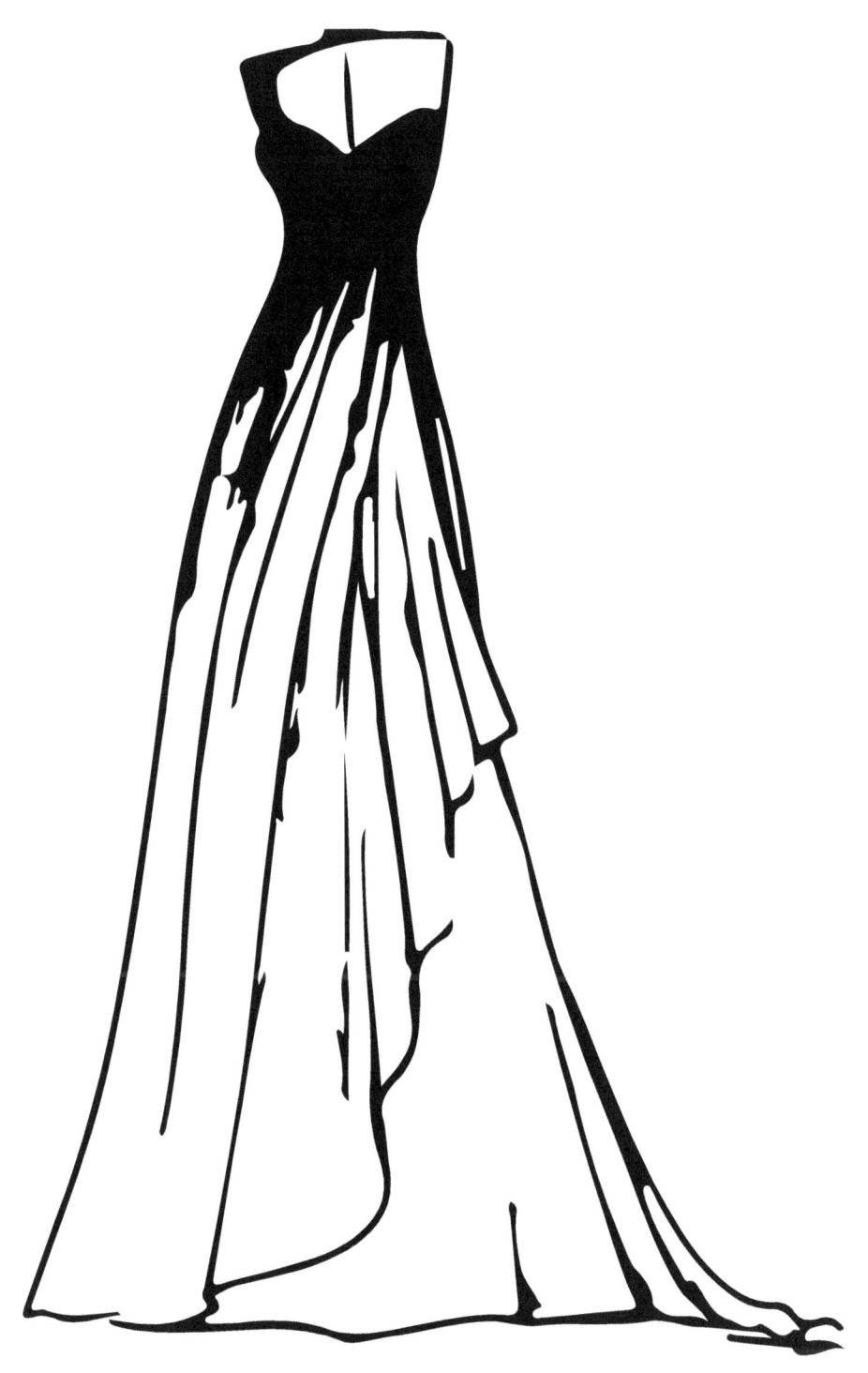

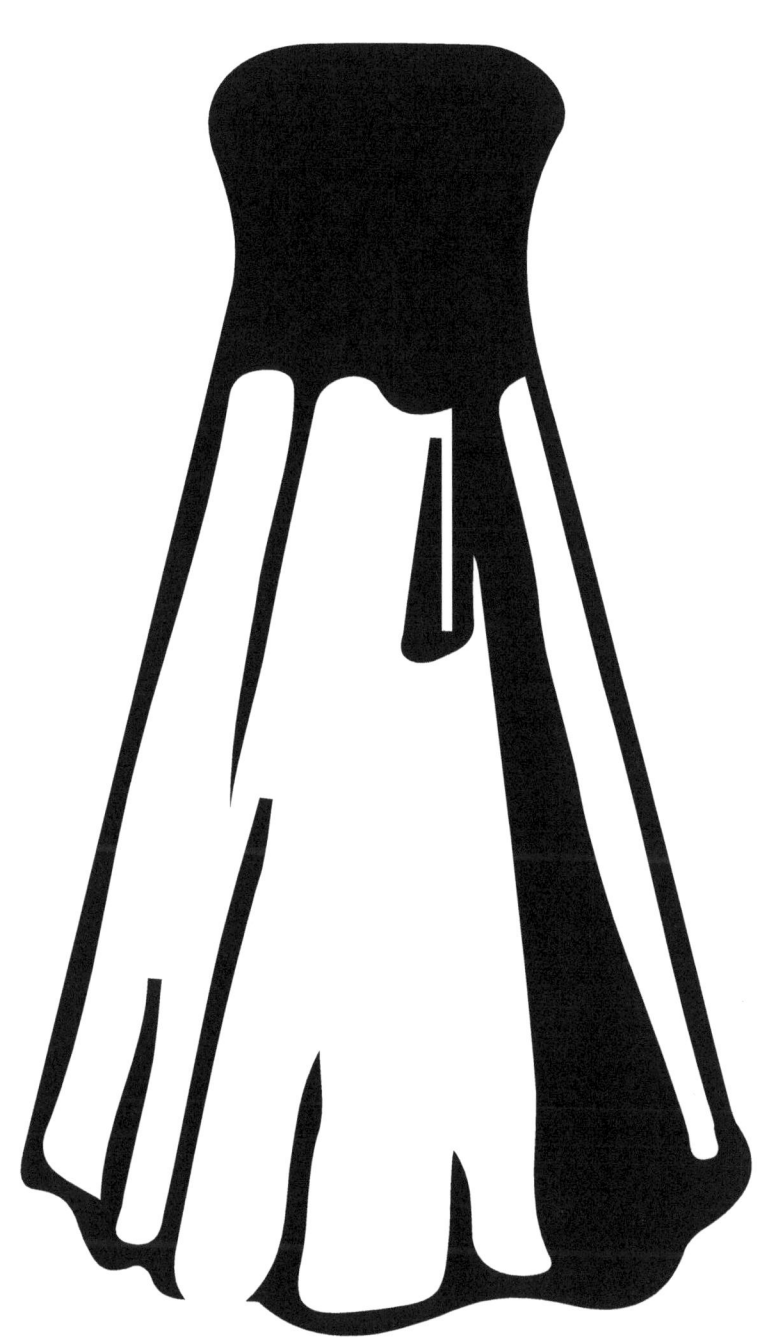